The Mayfly

Michael Ferguson Head

Edited by Rachael Mayer

authorHOUSE®

AuthorHouse™
1663 Liberty Drive
Bloomington, IN 47403
www.authorhouse.com
Phone: 1-800-839-8640

First published by AuthorHouse   07/12/2011

ISBN: 978-1-4634-2968-3 (sc)

Printed in the United States of America

Any people depicted in stock imagery provided by Thinkstock are models, and such images are being used for illustrative purposes only.
Certain stock imagery © Thinkstock.

This book is printed on acid-free paper.

The Mayfly

Table of Contents

For The Great Spirit

"A good poem is like a Mayfly . . . its ambiguity
outlasts its karma."

-MFH

Prologue

In a Moment

In the prodigal journey
Of spiral helixes
I fumble the road—
Love as I see it is
Hit the heart of a wonder
So perfectly kind
My roofs torn asunder
Axles do grind.
Please don't be perfect
Sunset to day
On the wings of thought
No shades of grey.
I feel like a circuit
Bursting divine
On heat sensations
His, hers, or mine.
These watts were something
Fitfully gained
Along certain sockets
Channels are changed.
Courage in a blackout
There is no switch.
The snake asks a question—
He idly sits.
Whatever the weather

Engage the rain
Turn it to sunshine—
Nature's to blame.

Spring

Come Forth by Tanya Rose

Taking a Breather

Green is the color of my fancy
As it waters
Colors of even more curiosity.
They're calling to me
With some method of beauty
That's almost criminal in nature—
The way it roils my senses.
How does it labor without lifting a finger
To almost run me off the road
With its integral offspring?
The tadpoles are mute
While their existence consistently
Swims a garden
Bloated with blessings
(As suns do judge).
My mind doesn't matter
When I'm bare-footing a stream
And my senses are straddled
Over two pebbles
No one else will ever see—
They remind me of grapes;
The stream smells of staunch algae.
Where were my problems now pressing?
They were clinging to my pores

Like barnacles.
I'm breathing now
But it's so unhindered
That it feels like a giant nothing—
Clean, bland, rampant.
It's so clear now
Now I can see
That I can't argue over something
That made great great for me.

The Watering Can

You push me into happiness
Like health into fever
That bleeds a thermometer toward heaven
Like helium
Spitting air into inconsequence
In habitual directions
Like rain, if it wanted to
But it's entirely too rebellious
And water has shadows
That hide in the noon
Like salamanders
Dodging hunger
When the sun's on stage
And the snakes are devout
Tanning on the road like beachgoers
On a margarita weekend
With old salts
Uncoiling the stress of the wilderness
That can say no
To the true
And sometimes render the efficacious
Like broken English
Because meaning turns on a swivel
If you water the human.

Engage the Tears with Caution

As it was
The weather beat us heavily
And the flowers cringed for a streak.
All around the pier the gulls chilled in perfect stasis
Like a taxidermist's picnic
And wild rice fell down from the sky that chapped the
boy
Out with us for a jaunt in Mother Nature's wrath.
Yellow was the color of my age—
Not the child who digs the flame
Or rocks away night with a heart's needle,
Damning the storm with every stride of his own
conflagration—
The corners of his eyes turned up
At the instance of any kind of normality's stipulation.
No, he was going to hit the truth face first
And come sliding down the bitter slopes of passage
Picking the scab of his hurt.
I blame stealth for the pain that nurtures love.
I came so far to quell the form of his fit
Like a ladybug's named by a man who loves,
Or a jacket on a breath-full night,
Zipper up, fear down,
Keeper of the locket around our hearts.

We engaged the tears with caution
And aimed for the shelter that brought us.
There's no name for where we lit for the calm
But it saved us for a spell
What poured down from hell
Only dreams exercised the boy's conscience.
His spirit was intact
But his eyes had two creases under half moons.

Cloven

The nakedness of her body
Was like a sharp and penetrating arrow
Volleyed into ether like a comet;
And the softness inside cuddled like the ocean
In its supple grasp
When the moon pulls it dangerously deeper into men
Not ready for the dawn's catalysis
Or the cold knife of spring
When nature's blind to its own loveliness—
The strawberry ineffable—
Deaf as a dog-whistle.
But her eyes were loud—
A blue that cursed its own limits
And stomped on my soul like an adolescent.
Her life was decidedly nuclear
But delicate in our radical symbiosis
Which generated time;
And she was true.
I thought the love that no one knows
So hard my brow was sweat;
And my heart fornicated with itself
Each time she touched me.
There was a night in the river of her hair
That found my star . . .
And clove it.

Oversleeping

The trembling veil of a dream
Groaned in my temples
Like a death-rattle—
Heathens mustn't think too hard
Or they'll sever.
I never can remember the steel grind
Of under-imagination
When my eyes taste the breath of oxygen
And the terror dissipates like a chance introduction
To people of no consequence—
Time's all a heap of broken images
That traces the back of my sticky eyeballs
With black chalk—
How many self-portraits till the end?
I'm flummoxed.
Dreams tame reality into robots
But the unconscious spreads like the spores of
dandelions.
The stage is so malleable—
Wonder is incurable—
Sleep has no fire-engines.

From There to There

Sensation being first
The tunnels of time have a radius that emits energy—
Where atoms are unhinged
And honey sticks
To the oldest question
(As a diamond has no effigy).
The Lord is speaking to us from nature
Through a loon's laryngitis
Sometimes on organic levels
Sometimes on spiritual planes
And hides His head like an ostrich
When chemistry comes.
It's about time the flowers had their say
In 'Manifest Destiny'.
They're rules in the way orbs turn
But the dreams for Mars need watering—
They're more attractive
Than a rose in a yellow dress
To a parched bee—
To us . . . his fear is his ephemeral victory;
With us . . . lives are too short:
The ability to cognate dampens;
Love is struck thousands of times

Until a desired drunkenness;
And darkness is just a word . . .
Light becomes a temporary encyclopedia.

Close to Catharsis

Children sketch tabula rasa's
Though clocks fall hard on their psyches
Like a shroud over mountains.
They labor over a litany of fresh urges
Or wrap themselves in gauze
When new people
And new responsibilities come knocking—
Even the lovely can scar.
Opportunity shoots the game of having to be
And its river runs further than they can see.
Hello kind sir,
Could you lend them a cheeseburger?
They're so close to another catharsis
They can taste the salt of another good day.
No compass to steer them right,
They use mother's intuition
To find father's invention—
The fattest enigma this planet knows;
It spreads like wildfire
In a child's brain
Coughing-up erudition
Where ignorance once festered like an infection—
And that exhaust is no laughing matter.
It puts out the lights of insecurity
And roughens-up still water.

They move forward now
With sturdy legs
To handle the question of Earth's rocking
And all that animals entail.
When life comes to them talking
They spit-up the blood of their hearts
Like rhubarbs.

No Way Out

Going down now
The moment is frighteningly real
At a pace that resembles gravity
But in two places:
My head and my heart.
These are the days of integrity
When friends are enemies;
And enemies are friends.
Down further I can see two loved ones
Exchanging heat and ideals
Abreast mountains of hypocrisy—
People run about thinking invisibility
When their hearts beat louder than bells
In and out of clouds and wells.
A mixing is a choice of two
That cognate like Christianity
But circle like Easterners
So they bridge like beavers—
There is no rest
Till they sign constitutions—
Seed that pistils revolutions,
Sometimes the unwelcomed guest.
But we can't escape the Earth's turn—
Stasis that the void learns—
Still.

Photograph

(A Song)

I took a picture of a bed of roses
And discovered the thorns were as big as our noses
And the only thing that I could do
Was develop the film and give it straight to you.

There are so many things that make iron cringe
Cause whether you know it or not were out on the fringe
The elevator is faster than the rich or the poor
When the weeds are greedy and the gardeners snore

No matter how many times they knock on the door
There's some good in this world; it's worth fighting for.
No matter how many times they knock on the door
There's some good in this world; it's worth fighting for.

I like that you are you and me are me
Cause happiness is the core, and gifts are so free
The ladybug was named by a man who desired
And the lovely in question was immediately hired

Sometimes the weather's lowly and the clouds are
strange
Meteorologists classify the constant change

But the sun comes out when we do our chores
The ill and dead of the past are not just lore.

No matter how many times they knock on the door
There's some good in the world; it's worth fighting for.
No matter how many times they knock on the door
There's some good in this world; it's worth fighting for.

Do, Do, Do . . . .

When She Did . . .

(*Based on Pride and Prejudice*)

Lizzie's a plain girl with striking features
In the twist of a world that catches colds
From snobby fools whose kitschy grants
Are stacked like bricks from the days of old;
Her sole quest to kick the "man" paints
The dynamics of her family's textures,
Curious to the gentry's bumbling ambitions—
Enough to enact an act of contrition
Between two attentions who dare to love—
When time prefers favorable marriages
From push to shove and ball to glove—
Without the greed for noble carriages,
When men perjure their names for their prey
And women flash their whites for a say
In a male-dominated society
In which Lizzie would rather be dawn's spinster
While maintaining her soul's sobriety
Than Madam to a man that could duly bind her—
The riddle that walked Hertfordshire.
If only he could weigh the honor and bias—
The one that stacks as high as she has
In the game of Austen's most complex novel;
She wrote in a time of ruthless war

Yet the gnawing question is not dead
As her fountain pen crashed and soared
How the hapless couple mends their thread
Without having to vex and needlessly gravel
The joy they find at the end instead—
Only what happens when a girl meets boy.
As neighbors it's incumbent for us to learn
We make sport of ourselves and them in turn.

Summer

Privy-Dunes-Sky by Tanya Rose

Southwest

When the wind blows southwest
It reminds me of the days
When Eric and I planed
Off the sea's milky platter
On his thirty-foot sloop
Where we went didn't matter
Where we went wasn't named
Jumping through life's hoop
In a medicinal haze
Off the salty, blue crest
To our own little world
God held us, and we were hurled
Intrepid we flew
On a sublime broad reach
A skipper and crew
In a tide like a leech
Burning in the apocalyptic sun
Setting the Genoa for a rollicking run
The more we skipped further
Youth gripped our souls
Traveling by the luff while the sea rolls and rolls
Wisdom is so relative
We chased it like the rain
We surfed God till the sun was lame
Those were rare days

And it helps to breathe
Any lovely mess the past conceives
Forever on our way
"Hiking" the snowing
A singeing sunrise is always glowing
I'm there too
Cap in hand
Ready for all a human can stand.

Berries

We stopped at Park St.—
The axle of public transportation
And I sweat a tear or two
Being the edgy type
But acutely motivated to learn every quest.
The heat wrestled the fans—
Large, metal scent propellers
That scattered the people like a broken vase—
They fell into the car in a deluge
When the doors were enticingly drawn.
There were more colors than a Kaleidoscope
More driven than drifted
Into awkward spaces
Or inertia's plight.
We started moving
To our secret destinations
Houses, cars, trees, and stations
(A stop that took longer than the turtle's cue).
My mettle was melting
As my pocket was all "Afghan"
And my nerves were popping like little fire-snaps—
The car . . . a typical head-case.
My salacious vapors
Must have been doing a little shakin'
Cause I saw you clenching a bar

Swimming your eyes in sweat
Cocking the love or the law at me like a cop;
Plucking my soul like a berry—
So chilly to be naked—
Suspicion so palpable.
We lit for the first stop
Where we could find a place for someone to . . .
Share themselves as berries do.

The Tacking Duel

He tacked to starboard again
Which vexed me thoroughly
But I rolled my hull over like jerking a stubborn mare
And kept her as flat as glass
As she continued to duel with the chiseled white-caps.
I meant to choke his wind into whispers
And cease soul's progress;
Blind him from the sun;
Hurt his mess.
The sun blustered to the point of unreason
But its fire illuminated my drive—
I was going to the start;
I was going to the finish . . . .
He didn't stay for long
And I found myself pumping to port again:
"Cover him like paper;
Cover before the land can make a shift" . . .
I was on my organic way.
We were like the undecided
Flirting with the ghost of a finish-line
Jamming so thick and articulate
It was almost dizzying.
My back was so gelled and my thighs were so tight
I could have been fiberglass.

The paranoia was loud
Like the hurt of a dead bell—
Where was he?
My head was tangential
As the intensity formed a cloud
Over my red chi
With blocks and luffs and sheets
Screaming a carnal shame.
The puffs hit like cries of import;
I chased them as far as my bow could point.
But the salt stung my eyes into interlopers
Holding briefly
As I knived the blue.
I prevailed the triangle
And left my opponent broken and stationary . . . .
The committee-boat let out one hoarse hail
Over the silky coat of wet air—
Chance made proud by fear.

Love's Uncompetition

Croquet at five with the children
Is a grand affair
Bordering on the comical.
The balls always seem to get lost
In a haze of prowling innocence.
The strokes are often ineffectual.
The wickets are quickly uprooted and thrown
Helter-skelter to the sky.
Then we promptly chase them
Around the yard making faces—
This is highly efficacious.
And when the sun splits its cherry
At night, we forget to pick up the pieces
For want of dinner and wine and family.
This is how croquet is played.

As He Slumbers

Happiness creeps through the corners
In the maid's quarters on cold and rainy nights
Like the patter of pigeons
And the moon is smothered in ash.
A safe and colorful feeling rests on the bed sheets
Like smoky tea on a tray of fine china
And I smell spring laundry percolating in the hamper
As if it had one day to confess its tangerine—
Whaffs of nectar and green grass turned fruit for the
chase of summer
Pruned from the original tree that haunts my backyard
Yawning in southwest breezes like a milked child—
There, where the clouds cast their shadows in my stone
eyes
And graded troughs of the sea—
Brute and whited as the monster that stirs inside.
I'm increasingly overwhelmed by the whip of music in the
air
Thrown from the mint voices
J-walking the corridor from the kitchen
Like a love concerto.
No one needs to know of the degree of my chakras
As I move towards the solstice
And the Earth sweats like a champion—
Rain like the sky's dander

Donning my home like socks
And tilling my heart with a dancer's panache
Only my soul opting for adventure . . .
Maybe tomorrow when God turns on his side.

Love's Misalliance

Just what exactly is in Van Gogh's stars? . . .
The ones we have if we choose to use them—
Brash and simple, but stultifying
Less a collective, more individual
Quite radical in its staid
While others move about in restlessness.
The key to a ball of turgid hydrogen
Is the flatulence of dreams—
They don't live a billion miles away
When they eat our eyes with conductivity.
They're a flash, a gleam, a fright,
Something so ineffable
We couple in a twist of fire
From the point of creation
To the burst of apocalyptic ejaculation.
Our minds croon like alley-cats
Because there is no answer in an answer.
There is no thought without nature's squeeze.
Boas rule the race
When the devil in a soul proceeds.
Be it without salvation
Or the conduct of continuation
We read the writing so small
In and out of a fiery ball.
Let the world come to Bethlehem

Or the wisdom of the "Indian".
It doesn't matter under a starry night
That we feel some delight
Because he was just a man
With the capacity for love's misalliance—
"I don't know you,
But I'm white-knuckled
From a fight
To water your sunflowers!"

Go!

Seeing through angel eyes
When fruit still teethes on ripeness
There's no one word for adventure
And eleven words for "go".
The reason for reasons is unattainable
And close in on the superfluous
Or did anyone know?
To be young and to be free
Melts like a love-chapped sundae
Down brash innocence
Daring to compile years of complicity—
A race is just a race
And love is so commonplace;
It's a given like gravity.
What marks this time
From this, that, or the other
Is written in hopscotch chalk
Washed away by the rain.

In the Sound

Waking on water from a mildewed cockpit;
Sun hacking the horizon in a troubled red
Like a blood-clot turning featureless, and gay.
Clouds are so shy and in jeopardy
Not one pokes a white plume;
And the wind's a dry razor—
Shave my wonder.

I'm so still
I feel the sloop skulking the waterline
Like a dolphin making forever in five knots.
Living the ocean's not an avocation;
It's restlessness.
I walk a rolling deck with abandon
And it makes love to me;
And I'm never who I am when I clip salt—
I am the underbelly of no distinction—
I am that same water . . . called nobody.

Then I haul the main;
It shivers like the hypothermic;
And the jib her little sister
Writhes in air not her own.
I make way rigged for an apocalypse
And the helm so heavy

Heaving the trail of an eastern rain
Like a necklace brushing my clavicles
Without occupancy.
Underway is an indictment of nature—
The luff prattles;
The spray slings water in a blink;
I jump over myself
Collecting speed like shells in the sand;
And the sea's a cold, wet stink—
Ungovernable.

I happen upon titillation
As the swells march across my paces
Like swilled rum.
I'm a dot in the ocean
Ready for God's explosion
And the wind's tale
Throwing old
Like the young.

Buzz

Stars chime Osirises
North of my rapid mind
In clusters of white violets
That stir endlessly
Now to now;
Cheat Zeus from his bolt
With the untold story
To bleat in an eye
Too sound to guide Joseph
And Mary's
Universal charge
Of church plucked from bone;
Cry euphemism?
When sisters and brothers
Lick sword from stone—
Shakespeare's stage turned weak?
Diamonds still gay—
Relic of sheen—
Gnaw self-doubt
Like yellow-eyed raptors;
Murder hitting its peak
In bird (nature's progress),
Peculiar dauntless—
Whipped thermals bray;
In and out of suns—

Lungs' wounded race;
I'm cringing from the heat
Love in my chest . . .
All the rest
Bleeds life wherever
And whatever
I'm being.

The Conundrum

On the eve of summer's end
The music of the air toils in the grass
Like seals flopping on the breast of Monomoy Point.
Whether or not autumn dies . . .
It's coming like a desert banshee.
Each trace of the moon is more salient than the next
When I have one night to live.
The people are suffocating in the gumdrops of their eyes
As if there were a cost to the sun's ascension.
These days are shrinking like firelight
After the story has been told.
And the children are rushing to their learning
Like foxes to their holes—
Where will they flock to when the rudimentary is over?
The answers are on the back of my eyelids.
All along the coast the gulls are crying wolf
Like a hundred creaking doors
Jabbering at a bonfire with closed beaks.
I'm the wolf, the job, and the conundrum—
Ceaseless in my journey to stab my heart for words.
On the clouds the gods are laughing at me
With my rearing compass
En route to my lovely—
Thick and bruised from my brainstorming—
Many lives some say.

And the hammer falls down
As I near my dying—
A new season can't shine without a little hurt.

Autumn

Down-Under-Within-Grass by Tanya Rose

Crash~Landing

I steward the landing-gear.
I float my life-raft.
It's me that gets the pummeling of the white-caps
When the ocean tries to swallow me and my mettle—
Chaste as orange juice.
But the salt remains my friend
From me to it
Or it to me
Distilling's just an art
However you be.

My Eye's Shepherd

My dog is loving her laze
And the wind is pushing the trees west
On account of nature's thorny breath
Heaving half-lives across a warm Cape lust—
A bleat desire to linger in the troughs of salt
Which engined centuries ago;
A trace of bitter drunkenness in the eye
And magic casting Cat-Boats further
Through the deaf of a sound
Whipped to the bone and waiting for the Blue to run like
firecrackers.
My pores were brine.

And the night falls kind
With the sun sacked by mist that moves,
My jaws open with love-braces
When the darkness dotes on my bosom;
And I hear the gong singing on her side—
All blind, all checked
Meeting under the moon—my eye's shepherd
Rearing its crescent through the ether
That stopped my heart when it called,
"Here is the sickle of my soul . . .
Take it and pray in your imagination."

I lost track of time when my body was lost
Cradled by a different sun
And stuffed my pride for an answer . . .
But the day came as the night idly slipped away.

It Stands

Inside it's kind of complicated.
I see salt and pepper sparring
With each other like two bums for another bottle
Of brute addiction.
However, the god's seize a truce
After nearly charring the strength of their myths.
The waters open; and an intrepid is born—
The wonder must conquer all
And if it doesn't
We settle Mars like the Puritans.
I'd like two hugs and a Corona with some stars raining
on top
And to go outside and lick until my fingers are like
rubber-cement
When I get the air situated for dream processing.
They'll be a christening like nuclear fireworks
And I can live with the water unknown
Bubbling in the strata like a pot on a gas stove,
Drink its new reality with open lips
And lullaby to football on a Sunday afternoon.
Gravity is a like warm cloth kissing the dress of my
flesh—
A cuddle is a cuddle and no less;
And it loves my lungs like the butt of a cigarette
Stealing the anxiety from my Mondays.

And errands press softly
Against my agenda:
The right; the wrong; and the rest
In time . . . all is forgiven, all is right, all is best;
And if it divvies
I rabbit the hole, settle Mars, raise my hand,
Tangling Yo-yo's from time to time—
When it can't walk . . . it stands.

Libra

The shape of a woman
Is inclined to take on various kinds of loveliness;
And that reality or idea
Jumps like the horny wrinkles in the blues of flat satin.
The strictures of time turn obsolete
And glee pours like rain from the mind—
Both of which are untraceable.
The kindness wrenches in a loop of flesh
Teetering on all possible titillation
That rubs the rest so soon
The senses roll in a bar of milky butter
And size sings with a wisp of vapor.
All that is touch now turns tangible
And the noon-bell rings its actuality.
Hordes of hair splash the eyes
As if to awaken some child of generating substance
In a man if he dares to call himself fire.
In all its illumination it sets a blaze in his whys . . .
But there is no dilemma in being.
A woman is his water,
She is the counterweight of his love—
Essential and ungovernable to all kinds.
Whether he swims or drowns is no matter
Because the sea goes in circles;
And men only live when they're dizzy.

Frost on THC

The only basket you can put all your eggs in is love.
The rest are highly questionable and need further study.
I'd multitask till I hit the total of a blowfish
But love is kind of giddy and I don't want to pop—
Or at not least yet.
There's too much to be done in the area of exploration—
I have weak shoulders from doing impressions of Atlas
Solely so I could run a little further every day.
It's tiring, but worth every bump or blister.
I'll quiet down someday
Like a bird that becomes hoarse
But these are days of severe interest.
Courting the moon is fine and all
But chapel is close to the day's stall—
Irony in the race of its tachometer.
I want to make a garden full of stars
And tend to the comets of a flower's equation—
The fruits of the "verse's" tree;
There need not be weeds growing in you and me.
Sleeping after this is peaceful thing
Like the cultured days of Austria—
The brain leaping into a pit of the unknown
Allowing what's under to breathe.
When dawn wakes for work I'll undress that apple
Quench, dance; come nerve and sing!

A Sip of Tea

Out there it's a kind of wonderland
And gravity seems to be a bit askew.
What's right is right.
So I went outside to huff a smoke—
Soak up the stars like Bounty
And get a perspective on the state of invention . . .
Was it cracking its whip that night?
Did the muses land on my head like a bucket of water?
I'd get an earful of information that defined my erring
character—
The one I jog all the way to town with
Mesmerized by the movies I make in my mind.
This was my whaffing chance.
In order for me to sip the snack of being human
I had to strip my inhibitions,
I had to walk where I would walk
Even if salvation was dangling at the end like a
strawberry,
Or the night was exceedingly overwhelming . . .
The clock was going to drop.
I tarried for a moment
And checked my wallet for such an expedition,
Knowing not that I already ripped its glassy wave—
It's the snake's venom that haunts my still water.

I fought hard over my brief name
And corrected my thoughts with the ancients,
Ten percent more than I could tell.
The science of truth and analytical thinking
Explained much of what I took in breath,
Except the slippery absence of meaning—
The book of hearts that no one's trumped.

Confronting Unreason

Arcane as it may be
The life of a bard
In hunting days
Wearing no coat of convention
Lacks a grand notion
Only splinters of perception
Haunt his absence of peace
Like grain in ale
Crying the luminously rank curls
Of God's blue beard;
Truth being so disgustingly sabbaticalized
He perambulates
Like a wounded stag
Atlas' abdomen
In shorn days
Trimmed of rectitude
And Oak leaves;
The delight of the Earth
Peaching on another horizon
Where love was pinched
Like a crystal quarter
Spent gluttonously on alien dreamers
With deep pockets—
Budded black holes in its cotton

Where he now threads
What might not have been said
With love now and lead.

Liability

Once, in a black hour
Jamie redistributed
His emotional cancer
To small bins
In order to pacify
Instances of clinically eclectic peace.
He hired bomb squads for his senses.
Life was much too scary
For the clockwork luminary
To souse his open nerve
With the jumping ordinary—
Jalapeño bright
Sense obliterating grenades
That ignited with a splash of wind
At sun stereotypes
Which fell out of little, cotton pockets
Like electric lint
Down to the fatherly ground
Blasting to ghastly contact
At which point
No one was held accountable
For the silent roar
Of that all too fantastic
Stirring without
And festering within.

On the Inside

The scrapes on his legs were meaningless
And the sound of his captors
Had petered out over the hills of discontent
On the steps of cowards
That lie in the face of lies—
Could scars be so familial?
There's no decent way to describe the event
Without the might of the bereft
And the weight of the whirled
That shadow this castled land
Where he sewed his soul
With plant, and sea, and stars.
The blood does not count
When it's bruised its amount
And the hurt is reinvested
In armored pursuit of its opposite day.
This is the time of the fruit—
What's given to him from the ground
Not the other way around.
He saw it not getting grey
At strange altitudes
Because it blossomed on the inside
When the sun wouldn't share rays.

Putting on Rubber Soul

I'm a sip of a mad fiddler.
My seed is bottomless and has knives that carve odes
Taunting the devil to eat out his occupation
With icy cognition replete with charm.

And the music shocked my spine
Like the pang of trout humping a river
Desperate to jet spawn and tumble virgin ears
With beats falling on rests—
England percolating in the sound like a jar of flies.

Bang and the soul is off like a bunny.
I hold myself as not to get lost—
The casualties of confusion are vast
When the imagination clots like beads of water
And drinking the clouds is sparse and highly
suspicious—
Only grit can win me back.

Singers rap cylindricals of utter nonsense
Through the doors of my edge-water,
And the phrases sink like rods down my innocence
Subtly like centipedes hopping through a row of tires
Raw as worms for bait

Lobbying for my consciousness—
What seemed like for hours
I flew my hedonism.

Winter

Psychotropic by Tanya Rose

Thanks for the Notepaper

Java at 6:00
When the winter begins to seep through the revolving
door
A coffee shop has ripe windows and jazz
Percolating its crispy nook
Shaking sleep from its milky eyes
Like a "Lab" in the throes of an ocean's friction—
All hints of Earth in the crease of time's ether
Swallowed by the jaws of an infinite "verse".
We're luckier than the laws of friendship—
Just a man and his coffee in a November tease
Flexing down the gullet in another awakening
To the sass of a city;
A whaff of hazelnut;
And the loveliest sip of the soul.
Only eagles see further
When the sun jockeys for the horizon
Like Mercury runs in a roll.
And we're off . . .
Dear to ourselves . . .
God-speed till the night palls . . .
Come let the day explain us.

The Storm

I can't shake the winter from my tail—
It's a snow-driven fever
Decimating my immune system
With cold Caterpillars
Never done
Till the snowflakes have won.
Where are my eyes?

My brain remembers taught evergreens
Here and there
Boasting impermeability—
White and white and white
Kissing spruce.

I lit candles in my room
Bleeding patchouli
As the wind buffed my windows
Shaking "gem-like flames".
Firedogs barely held me together.

I cried night down my cheeks
That stung like stars
And found my sight from snowflake to rain
Catching a glimpse of a storm

That was so vastly uncorrupted . . .
It came—
The genius of nature.

Clocks

Because in that clock was a storm
That couldn't be mollified with caution
Nor good intention.
It was menacing enough
That sweat stung my eyes with
Salt each second it stalked me—
Chalked with scorn and warm saliva.
Indeed, I was late for time
When there were no stops or allowances.
I just pushed air that had knowledge
And stalled hands with rougher hands.
Tardiness rained a discomfort
And lightning flashed a silence
Because even if I had arrived . . .
My head was never that far—
I was in a waste land
Late for life
Thus caught in the spell
Of an odyssey
That thought so hard
For me not to "tick" to you . . .
I heard it talk.
But clocks are just clocks
And time is entirely too linear.

12:00:01 a.m.

And the second-hand twitched
The hazelnut air
With a lactic exhaustion
That trespassed the halls of midnight
Cold
With the candor of shadows
Frequently alerting her to the presence of mist
That crawled like blood
All over the hallows of an ancient December
In the bloom of her life
That was her to her, and to her alone
A breakfast of loneliness
Like tides that cling to moons
When the sun is dead
And blackness stings her eyes like an electrification;
Buzz goes the mind
With epiphanies falling like chaff
From the illimitable song of the self—
Truth is the lie of beauty;
And she lies in the palm of night.

The Blue Café

Funny when I realized
I was walking backwards
Upside-down
And therefore straight ahead
To the blue café
Where I could properly sulk
When January is so bleak
At its peak
So much so that I had to dig into my pockets
For change that would better suit me
For the hot of your lovely
When I can't find anything
To protect me
From the illegality
Of our crush
Which realigns compasses
In the deepest caverns of the brain—
The driver of men's fates
That were so recently strong
I tripped over myself
Before the café was even illuminated.

The Transient

How odious I should think
The task of giving something a name—
We are the kinetic.
What *do I* know about things that move?
Brains run faster than cheetahs
And souls are anomalous—
Does *your* love have a color?
Can you stop clouds?
Nothing's always the same when I make lexicons.
God made me changeable;
My moods walk down long corridors
Without station;
They butter-up snowflakes
None like the other
Tendencies have no mother.
I'm peering through the glass
At myself on the other side . . .
Shaken.

Definition

Winter tramples a surfeit
Of snow-pedestrians
Like shiny dirt
Rankling in their coarse tweed
Across ages
Of cold alabaster
Like caffeine-caterpillars
Searching for meaning
In a fist full of dust;
And in that star
My crunchy ice-heart
Melts in globs of greedy light
All over time
Like a love-chapped sundae—
Hands inching always
Toward the gleaming, metal slot
Of poetic ignition:
An eternally obscure mission
Yielding angular ink spots
Of lie-leaking truth
In brevity.

Cabin Fever

For days now the wind has battered my cottage;
The cracks in my clapboard have howled at fuzzy moons
There's no telling when my heart will break
If it continues its vitriol
But my fingers are crossed in iron cuffs
And my brows are beating by the fireside.
My foundation groans at the northern puffs . . .
Near now.
Something wicked strokes my feathers
Free of charge;
It stalks me without mercy.
I'll need dreams to carry me
Through nature's writhing breath
To a hiding place
Where I throw silent parties
And quench the fury of my grappling fists.
The gods pray me to brave the storm
I see it in my sleep when the blackness roams
(And conscious if the mood strikes me).
They're devils that whistle in the stovepipe;
I hear them when the wind jackknifes my nooks
Or when the witch is barnstorming my mind
And finds my terror for the unknown.
But there's rain on my domain;
I reel towards evil

Till I can't breathe the smoke of Hell
Anywhere but the part that's in me.
It's the other part that fuels me with grit—
I cure my saltbox.

For the Benefit of the Wicca

It was a new moon on the Winter Solstice
Icicles clung to the gutters like infants
And the ladies of the night moved in secret directions
Around a town that was so recently called "nothing"
Only fixtures of trees and lochs and farms and hands
Bled by the trough of the pitch sky
And rankled like the fur of a porcupine.
Pentacles were traced and traceless
To the non-believers who wore jackets of pure innocence
Tossed up like salad for the ceremonies
Of white and white—
The usurpers of love for love
While the creatures danced pyres with the movement of
magic
Called-up for the manipulation of man
And his theretofore misunderstood mind
Charmed like the Irish in boggling ways
The spells flew through morning sight
When the women returned to you and me
Like cats with eyes of fire.
The equinox was heel upon heel
And the half-light reeked prodigious
For those who used instead of loved—
A lady who sexes like a ghost never conceives
But idly relieves

Her penchant for being real—
She moves with the flow
But never knows
The potential of her living name.
Wake up and grab love by the mane!

"Indian Guides"

They sat in a circle of fathers and sons
Elaborating on the importance of a feather
In a darkly lit room full of shadows and memories;
Yet they were the present and *in* the present
As an eagle knows the wind.
Imparting knowledge is like a traveling merry-go-round
But wisdom has no wheels;
It gives as much as it steals.
These are the lungs of the Lake Forest Tribe;
Harvest Moons have nothing to hide.

Time stalked them in fruitful ways;
They told how scouts earn their trade;
Ingratiate the tools that honor the weather;
Smoke the pipe that brings us together;
Every sunrise tells you this;
Beware of Trickster's hit or miss.
This was before the stars were thrown insane
Or the liquor of the white man came.
Medicine, brave, chief, or warrior
There's never an end to the story or
We just tell it again
And trust the buffalo come again.
He's Little River, she's Red Dove, and that's Painted Tree
Little Big Thundercloud came to me.

Epilogue

Mental Note

Dear Subconscious,

       Thank you for the kind invitation,
      Yet I am unable to attend the festivities this
evening. Give my best to the unraveling oceans.

                        Love,

                            Mike

Acknowledgements

I would like to thank Rachael Mayer for her help editing this book with such insight, precision, and accuracy. She has flawless taste and deserves much praise for her talents as a daring and unabashedly unique poet as well. She resides with her family in New England and continues her art, spreading her talent and the achievements of a long line of creative relatives.

I would like to thank Tanya Rose for her one-of-kind painting and photography that has helped set the mood and attraction of this book and poetry in general which has been sorely overlooked in many ways for decades. Her art can be seen at: shadowandsoul@verizon.net; shadowandsoul@deviantart.com; and Facebook.com under Tanya Rose.

I would lastly like to thank the publishing firm AuthorHouse for their attentiveness and patience in creating this book. They have fine means to launch essential literature none have or will have ever seen before.